KU-393-706

EARTH IN DANGER!

Coasts

Polly Goodman

HODDER
Wayland

an imprint of Hodder Children's Books

Schools Library and Information Services

S00000671179

Titles in the **EARTH IN DANGER!** series

Coasts   Rivers

Energy   Settlements

Farming   Transport

For more information on this series and other Hodder Wayland titles, go to www.hodderwayland.co.uk

This book is a simplified version of the title *Coasts* in Hodder Wayland's 'Earth Alert' series.

Language level consultant: Norah Granger
Editor: Belinda Hollyer
Designer: Jane Hawkins

Text copyright © 2001 Hodder Wayland
Volume copyright © 2001 Hodder Wayland

JUDLEY PUBLIC LIBRARIES
L 47971
671179   9CH
J 551.45

First published in 2001 by Hodder Wayland,
an imprint of Hodder Children's Books.

This paperback edition published in 2005

All rights reserved. Apart from any use permitted under UK copyright law, this publication may only be reproduced, stored or transmitted, in any form, or by any means with prior permission in writing of the publishers or in the case of reprographic production in accordance with the terms of licences issued by the Copyright Licensing Agency.

Britian Library Cataloguing in Publication Data
Goodman, Polly
Coasts. - (Earth in danger!)
1.Coasts - Juvenile literature 2. Coastal ecology - Juvenile literature
I.Title
333.9'17
ISBN 0 7502 4727 4

Printed in China by WKT Company Limited

Hodder Children's Books
A division of Hodder Headline Limited
338 Euston Road, London NW1 3BH

Picture acknowledgements
Cover: main picture Schafer & Hill/Still Pictures, coastline Edward Parker; Aerofilms Limited 7; Axiom Photographic Agency (Jim Holmes) 25; Chapel Studios (Zul Mukhida) 6; James Davis Travel Photography 10, 17; Ecoscene (Wayne Lawler) 13; Robert Estall Photo Library 18; Eye Ubiquitous (Tim Hawkins) 1, (M. Allwood-Coppin) 3, 8–9, (Pauline Thornton) 5, (Bob Gibbons) 8, (Paul Seheult) 26, (Paul Thompson) 28; Getty Images (Art Wolfe) 4–5, (David Olsen) 19, (Nigel Press) 20, (David Woodfall) 22; Horsehead Wetlands Center, 27 (both); Impact Photos (Javed A Jafferji) 12, (Simon Grosset) 14, (Mark Henley) 15, (Piers Cavendish) 21, (Rives/Cedri) 23; RSPB Images 11; Topham Picturepoint 16, 24.
Artwork by Peter Bull Art Studio.

Contents

What are coasts?

Coasts are areas of land next to the sea. They are important places. Most of the world's people live on or near coasts. Coasts are also home to many different plants and animals.

Coasts have different natural shapes. Bays and beaches have formed where the sea has worn away soft rock. Where there is harder rock, steep cliffs have formed.

A long beach on an island in the Pacific Ocean.▼

Rivers at coasts

Where rivers meet the sea they form estuaries or deltas.

An estuary is a place where a river meets the sea. The tides go in and out, covering and uncovering land in an estuary.

Deltas are flat, triangular areas of land near a coast, where a river splits into many channels. They form as rivers drop fine mud, called silt, on the land as they reach the sea.

TIDES

Tides are the rise and fall of the sea. They are controlled by the moon.

High tide is when the water is at its highest point on the shore.

Low tide is when the water is at its lowest point.

▲ Only plants and birds can live on steep cliffs like this one.

Changing coasts

Coasts are always changing. Strong waves and winds constantly wear away rocks. Whole beaches can be washed away by storms.

Some bays gradually fill up with silt dropped by rivers. The bays get more and more shallow until new land is formed. However, the fastest changes to coasts are made by people.

▲ This beach is being worn away by waves and the wind.

Activity

YOUR COAST

Look at a map of your region, and find out where the nearest coast is. If you live near a coast you could measure the distance from your school. Then describe the coast near you, by answering the following questions:

● Is there a beach or cliffs?
● Is there a village, town or city on the coast?
● What types of boat arrive at the coast?
● Are there roads or railways along the coast?

A TOWN UNDER THE SEA

Dunwich is a small village in Suffolk, on the east coast of England. It used to be the tenth-largest town in England. But today, most of the old town is under the sea.

In the eleventh century, Dunwich had many houses and large churches. By the fourteenth century, waves had begun washing away the cliffs at the edge of the town. Houses and other buildings fell into the sea.

Now the coast at Dunwich is 800 metres further inland than it used to be.

The ruins at the bottom of the photo are the only buildings left from the old town of Dunwich. ▼

Animals and plants

Coasts are important places for many plants and animals. For some, coasts are permanent homes. For others they are just resting places.

Sea birds spend much of their time catching fish in the sea. But in between fishing trips, many rest on the shore. Some sea birds breed their young on the shore, and feed them with fish.

◀ Sea lions on the Galapagos Islands.

The shoreline

The shoreline is the area between high and low tide. Plants and animals that live there are specially suited to living both in and out of the water.

When the tides go out, shellfish such as mussels and oysters attach themselves tightly on to rocks. Their hard shells stop their bodies drying out.

Shorelines provide a feast for birds when the tides go out. Where mud flats and rock pools are uncovered, birds can pluck out insects and fish with their beaks.

RICH PICKINGS FOR BIRDS

One cubic metre of mud in an estuary provides birds with as much energy as there is in twelve chocolate bars.

Sea birds called gannets rest on the shore in South Africa. ▼

River estuaries

Estuaries are broad mouths of rivers where salt water from the sea meets the fresh river water. The water in estuaries rises and falls as the tides wash in and out.

Estuaries are home to lots of different plants and animals. Plants grow easily in the shallow water because the sunlight they need can reach the bottom.

◀ Fish called mustard rays in a mangrove swamp in Ecuador.

Natural cleaners

Some plants in estuaries are natural cleaners. Beds of reeds purify water for plants and animals. They even clean water polluted by people, so that it does not harm the environment.

REST STOPS

Estuaries and beaches provide ideal resting places for migrating birds.

Sanderlings are birds that breed in the Arctic. At the end of the short summer, food runs out. So the sanderlings have to spend the winter somewhere else. They fly south, all the way to the coast of West Africa. The following spring they fly back to the Arctic.

The journey is too far to make without stopping. So the sanderlings rest on beaches and estuaries along the way. If these areas are built over by people, the birds will lose their feeding grounds and starve.

▲ Sanderlings on a beach.

People and coasts

Coasts have always been very important places for people. They provide food from the sea and from the land. They are also used for transport and trade.

COAST HOMES
By the year 2025, 75 per cent of the world's people will live on or near coasts.

Fish

People have hunted fish at sea for thousands of years. There are still important fishing ports on many coasts.

Fish are also farmed in ponds and tanks. Fish farming is big business on many coasts today because tonnes of fish can be produced and sold.

In warm countries, large areas of mangrove forest are destroyed when fish ponds are made. In cold countries, salmon are grown in tanks in the sea water.

◀ Fishermen putting out a net to catch fish.

SHRIMP FARMING IN ECUADOR

Shrimps breed in the sea near the coast of Ecuador, in South America. But people make more money by raising the fish in large ponds along the coast. When the ponds are made, large areas of mangrove trees are cleared away.

After a few years, the ponds fill up with waste from the shrimps. They are so crowded that many shrimps catch diseases and die. New ponds are dug further along the coast. This destroys more mangrove trees, and uses up natural places where fish breed.

▲ A fish pond in Ecuador.

Farming on land

Flat land near coasts is good for farming crops and animals. The soil in river deltas is very fertile, because when the river floods, it leaves rich mud on the land around it.

In the Netherlands, new farmland has been made near coasts. Walls, called dykes, have been built around land that is uncovered at low tide. The walls keep out the sea, and ditches drain water away.

Farmland on the coast of New Zealand. ▼

Transport and trade

Before aeroplanes were invented, people travelled between countries by ship. So coasts were important places for transport and trade.

Because coasts were good trading places, many settlements grew up there. Cities such as New York, Sydney and Tokyo grew up in natural harbours. These protected ships from strong winds and waves.

Many natural harbours are now busy ports, with factories and warehouses, airports and roads, offices and houses. Bulky goods such as coal and oil are loaded and unloaded there from big ships.

▲ A busy port in Hong Kong.

First homes

In the past, when explorers or settlers went to new countries, the first places they came to were coasts. In the 1500s, Europeans sailed to North and South America and settled on the coasts before they moved inland.

In the nineteenth and twentieth centuries, millions of people migrated, or moved to new countries to live. For example, people moved from Europe to the USA, and from Britain to Australia. Many people did not move away from the coasts where they first arrived.

People arriving in Britain from the Caribbean in 1958. ▼

Tourism

Coasts are good tourist attractions because people can do lots of different activities, such as swimming, windsurfing or kite-surfing.

Many coasts also have blue seas, sandy beaches and coral reefs for people to enjoy. Many people fly thousands of kilometres to visit coasts in other countries.

▲ A beach in Hawai'i.

Activity

TOURISM SURVEY

1. Collect a holiday brochure from a travel agent and choose a country.
2. Find the holiday destinations listed in the brochure, on a map. (The brochure will probably have a map in it.)

● Where are most of the holidays?
● How would you travel to the country?
● How far away is it?

Threats

Coasts everywhere are being damaged by people. Sometimes it is hard to see the damage we do, especially if it happens over a long time.

Areas of coast that might look like wasteland are usually home for many plants and animals. They may also do an important job. Sand dunes and cliffs protect the land from flooding when there are high tides or storms. Reed beds clean our water.

Many plants and animals depend on this river estuary. ▼

New buildings

New building projects change a coast for ever. Plants and animals lose their habitat. Fish lose their breeding grounds. The area may lose its natural defences against flooding. There is often pollution and rubbish from the new building work.

▲ A marina in San Diego, USA, with boats, shops, offices and homes.

This satellite photograph shows the huge delta of the Nile river, in Egypt. ▶

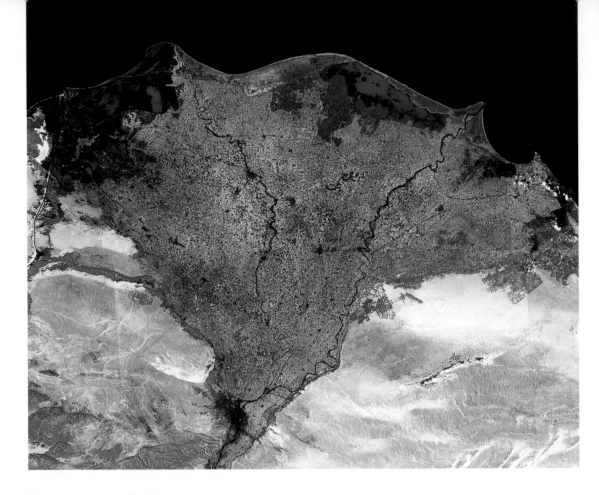

Rivers and dams

Coasts are also damaged by things that happen further inland. Pollution from industry and from farming goes into rivers, and is carried down to coasts. Water pollution kills plants and animals in estuaries.

Dams change the natural flow of rivers. They can stop rivers carrying silt to deltas, so the soil in deltas gets less fertile. Then farmers in deltas find it harder to grow food.

Dams can also stop nutrients being carried down to estuaries by rivers, so new-born fish have less food. If fewer fish breed in estuaries, there are fewer fish at sea for us to catch and eat.

Tourism

Tourist developments often damage coasts. New hotels, roads and shops cause pollution and rubbish. New tourist resorts can also destroy an area's natural beauty.

Pollution

Many coasts have been damaged by pollution. One kind of pollution is sewage. In many parts of the world, sewage is pumped straight into the sea without being treated first. The sea can only break down small amounts of sewage. So in these places the water around coasts is polluted.

Tourists on a beach in Japan. ▼

Chemicals

Chemicals used in homes, offices, factories and farms are washed into the sea by rivers. They pollute the water, killing plants and animals and destroying their habitat.

RUBBISH

Rubbish and pollution dropped on coasts can be carried thousands of kilometres away. The rubbish listed below was found on Ducie Atoll. This is a group of islands in the South Pacific where there are no people. The nearest place where people live is 5,000 kilometres away.

171 glass bottles from fifteen countries
113 sea markers
74 bottle tops
25 shoes
14 crates
7 drink cans
6 light tubes
1 toy aeroplane
2 dolls' heads
2 ballpoint pen tops

▲ Sewage washed up on swimming beaches is unpleasant and unhealthy.

OIL SPILL IN KUWAIT

During the Gulf War, between 1990 and 1991, soldiers from Iraq deliberately opened tanks containing oil in Kuwait. The oil spread along the Persian Gulf coast in a huge slick, many kilometres long. About 30,000 sea-birds were immediately killed by the oil.

The oil polluted marshes, mangrove swamps and coral islands along the coast, which are breeding areas for fish. There are now fewer fish in the sea because of the oil spill.

▲ A barrier tries to stop the oil spreading further in the Persian Gulf.

Climate change

Some scientists believe the world's climate is changing. They believe this is caused by burning fossil fuels such as coal, gas and oil, which we use to make electricity and run machines. When fossil fuels are burned they release gases into the atmosphere. This could slowly change the world's temperature.

If the climate did get warmer, huge areas of ice in the Arctic and Antarctic would melt, and sea levels would rise. Areas near coasts would flood more easily and some islands would be completely covered.

Melting icebergs in the Antarctic. ▼

In a warmer climate, many homes would be at risk from flooding. Countries with low coasts, such as the Netherlands and Bangladesh, would have to build expensive walls to protect against floods.

Mud flats and estuaries would become permanently covered by water. This would destroy the habitat for plants and animals. Wildlife that couldn't adapt quickly enough would die out.

▲ A flood in Bangladesh.

Activity

OIL SPILL

Find out what happens when oil is spilled in water, and how best to clean it up.

1. Half fill a jam jar with water and stir in some salt.
2. Pour some cooking oil into the jar so about 1 cm floats on top of the water.
3. Fasten the lid tightly and shake well.
4. What happens to the oil? Try clearing it up using a spoon and cotton wool. Which works best?

Protecting coasts

Coasts are important places for people, plants and animals. But it is easy for people to spoil coasts, especially if they do not realize how important they are.

In Florida, in the USA, about 30 hectares of natural wetlands are lost every day because of new building work.

Many countries are trying to make more people understand how important coasts are. Information centres and noticeboards display information about the different plants and animals that live along a coast. Tourists are asked to help take care of beaches.

◀ This sign in Thailand asks tourists not to stand on coral or drop litter in the sea.

CHESAPEAKE BAY

Chesapeake Bay is on the east coast of the USA. Many rivers flow into the bay and it is home for hundreds of species of wildlife.

▲ Children at the visitors' centre.

Since 1976, laws have been passed to try to protect the bay. The laws control how people get rid of waste in the area, and the types of fish that can be caught.

A visitors' centre has huts and towers where people can watch birds and animals on the bay.

Students study the wildlife in the bay. ▶

Conservation

Many coastal areas are being turned into conservation areas or nature reserves. New building projects are not allowed and the areas are kept as natural as possible.

Nature reserves are usually beautiful places where visitors can watch wildlife. Visitors have to follow certain rules, so they do not disturb the wildlife.

In some countries, before new building projects are allowed, scientists make a study of the area. They give advice about how to build the project so that it does not cause too much damage.

Coastlines like this one need to be protected so that visitors do not damage them. ▼

Activity

Look at this drawing of a coastline.

1. List the natural things you can see, such as beaches and cliffs.

2. List the different jobs people could do, such as fishing.

3. Which areas could be made into conservation areas?

Glossary

Conservation Looking after a natural area or material to save it for the future.

Defences Materials that protect against damage or attack.

Environment Everything in our surroundings: the earth, air and water.

Estuaries Places where a river meets the sea.

Fertile Something that is rich and productive.

Flood When a large amount of water covers land that is usually dry.

Habitat The natural home of a plant or animal.

Marshes Low land that is almost always covered by shallow water.

Migrating Moving from one place to another.

Nutrients Things that feed plants, animals and people.

Pollution Damage to air, water and land by harmful materials.

Ports Places where ships stop to load or unload people or goods.

Settlers People who go to a new place to live.

Sewage Liquid waste that is carried away from homes.

Shoreline The shoreline is the area between high and low tide.

Tides The rise and fall of the sea on the shore.

Wetlands Areas of low land that are covered by shallow water for much of the year.

Further information

TOPIC WEB

MUSIC
- Coastal sounds: birds, waves, ships
- Music associated with coasts, such as Fingal's Cave

GEOGRAPHY
- Landforms and processes
- Human use of coasts
- Land reclamation
- Nature conservation
- Environmental issues: global climate change and sea level, tourism, overfishing, pollution
- Population topics

HISTORY
- Migrations of people and religions
- Changes of coasts over time

ART & CRAFT
- Using coasts as a stimulus for drawing, painting and modelling

DESIGN AND TECHNOLOGY
- Coastal building or defences
- Land reclamation
- Pollution control

MATHS
- Measuring angles of slopes, the length of coasts or the height of cliffs
- Simple statistics

SCIENCE
- Ecosystems
- Biodiversity
- Adaptation to environment
- Ecological niches
- Food chains
- Environmental issues: e.g. habitat loss, water pollution, damage to ecology

ENGLISH
- Using coasts as a stimulus for creative writing
- Appropriate poetry
- Library skills

Other books to read

Earth Files: Oceans by Anita Ganeri (Heinemann, 2003)

Earth's Changing Landscape: Changing Coastlines by Philip Steele (Franklin Watts, 2003)

The Earth Strikes Back: Water by Pamela Grant and Arthur Haswell (Chrysalis Education, 2004)

Our Earth: Coasts and Islands by Terry Jennings (Belitha, 1999)

Geography Fact Files: Coastlines by Michael Kerrigan (Hodder Wayland, 2004)

Natural Disaters: Floods and Tidal Waves by Terry Jennings (Belitha, 1999)

Saving our World: Oceans by J. Parker (Franklin Watts, 2003)

Survivor's Science: at Sea/on an Island by Peter Riley (Hodder Wayland, 2003)

The World Reacts: Flood by Paul Bennett (Chrysalis Education, 2003)

What are...? Coral Reefs, Islands by Clare Llewellyn (Heinemann, 2001)

Index